PAELLA

PAELLA

40 DELICIOUS SPANISH-STYLE RECIPES

Design concept by Fiona Roberts
Produced by the Bridgewater Book Company Ltd
New photography by David Jordan
New photography home economist by Jacqueline Bellefontaine

Notes for the Reader

This book uses imperial, metric, or US cup measurements. Follow the same units of measurement throughout; do not mix imperial and metric. All spoon measurements are level: teaspoons are assumed to be 5 ml, and tablespoons are assumed to be 15 ml. Unless otherwise stated, milk is assumed to be whole, eggs and individual vegetables such as potatoes are medium, and pepper is freshly ground black pepper. Recipes using raw or very lightly cooked eggs should be avoided by infants, the elderly, pregnant women, convalescents, and anyone suffering from an illness.

Picture acknowledgment

The Bridgewater Book Company would like to thank Taesam Do/Foodpix/Getty Images for permission to reproduce copyright material for the endpapers.

Introduction

WHO CAN RESIST THE ENTICING AROMA AND MOUTHWATERING TASTE OF PAELLA? DELICIOUS GOLDEN RICE, TEMPTING MORSELS OF MEAT, POULTRY, FISH, AND VEGETABLES, AND TANTALIZING SPICES AND HERBS—THIS IS THE WEALTH OF WONDERFUL INGREDIENTS THAT SPRINGS TO MIND WHEN WE THINK ABOUT THIS FABULOUS DISH.

But where did paella come from? Depending on where you are in the world, you will hear different stories about the origin of this now internationally renowned dish. The Spanish province of Valencia is most often credited with being the home of paella. Each cook in this region seems to have his or her own idea of which ingredients are included in the authentic Paella Valenciana, and you will find one popular version in this book.

Since the Moors ruled much of Spain for hundreds of years, the Arabs unsurprisingly also have their own theory relating to the origin of paella. They say that paella was developed from the Arabic word *baqiyah*, meaning "leftovers." When Spain was under Moorish rule, poor fishermen who worked for the rulers were allowed to take home any food left over from banquets. The remains of fish, chicken, and rice dishes were mixed together on the spot, carried away, and then other ingredients were added at home. The Poor Man's Paella in this book celebrates this concept—a colorful and flavorful concoction of leftover meat and vegetables.

Wherever paella truly originated, one thing is clear—this great dish has now been claimed by the world, and is evolving all the time with new and inspiring combinations. This book features a selection of these exciting and innovative paellas, together with variations on the classics, for you to enjoy in your own home.

One of paella's most valuable qualities is its flexibility. Apart from the delicious base of golden fried rice, the combinations of other ingredients are truly endless, and you can vary them according to what you have available. Many paellas follow a specific "theme"—for example, majoring on seafood, with a variety of fresh fish and shellfish, or vegetarian, with beans or nuts and a mixture of fresh vegetables. Others mix meat, seafood, and vegetables together, for a rich medley of flavors.

Whichever combinations you choose, the rice base of the paella is essential. It is best to use a medium-grain paella rice, such as calasparra or bomba, because these are starchier than standard long-grain rice and help to give the paella its wonderful creamy consistency. If it is unavailable, use a short-grain risotto rice, such as arborio, instead.

SIMPLY INSPIRATIONAL

Unlike risottos, which are stirred constantly, the traditional paella is not stirred once the stock has been poured in—the pan is simply shaken from time to time. This method enables a delicious light "crust" to form on the bottom of the paella, which in Spain is known as the *socarrat*, and is the mark of a well-made paella. Getting the socarrat to form is not difficult, but it does require vigilance. Simply cook the paella, without stirring, until all the liquid has been absorbed, and you can detect a faint "toasty" smell coming from the rice—this indicates that the socarrat has formed. Remove the pan from the heat immediately, before the rice has time to burn, and cover it. Let stand for five minutes, then enjoy the paella straight from the pan!

SERVES 4–6

½ tsp saffron threads
2 tbsp hot water
8 oz/225 g tomatoes
5½ oz/150 g cod fillet, skinned
5½ cups simmering fish stock
   or water
12 large raw shrimp, shelled and
   deveined

1 lb/450 g raw squid, cleaned and
   cut into rings or bite-size pieces
   (or use the same quantity of
   shelled scallops)
3 tbsp olive oil
1 large red onion, chopped
2 garlic cloves, crushed
1 small fresh red chili, seeded
   and minced

1⅝ cups medium-grain paella rice
1 tbsp chopped fresh parsley
2 tsp chopped fresh dill
salt and pepper
1 lemon, cut into wedges, to serve

Seafood Paella with Lemon and Herbs

Peeling tomatoes makes them easier to digest and avoids having the smooth texture of the paella spoiled by detached tomato skins. Put them in a heatproof bowl, then cover with boiling water and let soak for 3 minutes. Drain, then cover with cold water, and drain again. The tomatoes will now be cool enough to handle and the skins will be easy to remove.

• Put the saffron threads and water in a small bowl or cup and let infuse for a few minutes. Peel the tomatoes (see note, left), then cut into wedges and set aside. Rinse the cod under cold running water, then add to the pan of simmering stock and cook for 5 minutes. Using a slotted spoon, transfer the cod to a colander. Rinse under cold running water and drain. Add the shrimp and squid to the stock and cook for 2 minutes. Meanwhile, cut the cod into chunks, then transfer with the other seafood to a bowl and set aside. Let the stock simmer.

• Heat the oil in a paella pan or wide, shallow skillet and cook the onion over medium heat, stirring, for 2–3 minutes, or until softened. Add the garlic, chili, and saffron and its soaking liquid and cook, stirring constantly, for 1 minute. Add the tomato wedges and cook, stirring, for an additional 2 minutes.

• Add the rice and herbs and cook, stirring constantly, for 1 minute, or until the rice is glossy and coated. Pour in about 5 cups of the hot stock and bring to a boil. Reduce the heat and let simmer, uncovered, for 10 minutes. Do not stir during cooking, but shake the pan once or twice. Season to taste with salt and pepper, then shake the pan and cook for an additional 10 minutes, or until the rice grains are plump and almost cooked. If the liquid is absorbed too quickly, pour in a little more hot stock, then shake the pan to spread the liquid through the paella. Do not stir it in. Add the cod, shrimp, and squid and shake the pan, but do not stir. Cook for an additional 2 minutes.

• When all the liquid has been absorbed and you detect a faint toasty aroma coming from the rice, remove from the heat immediately to prevent burning. Cover the pan with a clean dish towel or foil and let stand for 5 minutes. Serve direct from the pan with the lemon wedges to squeeze over the rice. Alternatively, divide the paella between warmed plates and serve with the lemon wedges.

SERVES 6–8

16 live mussels

½ tsp saffron threads

2 tbsp hot water

generous 1¾ cups medium-grain
   paella rice

about 6 tbsp olive oil

6–8 unboned, skin-on chicken thighs,
   excess fat removed

5 oz/140 g Spanish chorizo sausage,
   casing removed, cut into ¼-inch/
   5-mm slices

2 large onions, chopped

4 large garlic cloves, crushed

1 tsp mild or hot Spanish paprika,
   to taste

3½ oz/100 g green beans, chopped

generous ¾ cup frozen peas

5 cups fish, chicken, or
   vegetable stock

16 raw shrimp, shelled and deveined

2 red bell peppers, halved and
   seeded, then broiled, peeled,
   and sliced

salt and pepper

1¼ oz/35 g fresh parsley, minced,
   to garnish

Chicken and Shrimp Paella

The first time you make this, preheat the oven to 375°F/190°C while the paella simmers. Heat sources are inconsistent on stoves, so it is hard to say how long it takes for the liquid to be absorbed. If there is too much liquid on the surface, put the dish in the oven, then cover and bake for 10 minutes, or until very little liquid remains.

• Soak the mussels in lightly salted water for 10 minutes. Put the saffron threads and water in a small bowl or cup and let infuse for a few minutes. Meanwhile, put the rice in a strainer and rinse in cold water until the water runs clear. Set aside.

• Clean the mussels by scrubbing or scraping the shells and pulling out any beards that are attached to them. Discard any with broken shells or any that refuse to close when tapped. Set aside.

• Heat 3 tablespoons of the oil in a 12-inch/30-cm paella pan or ovenproof casserole. Cook the chicken thighs over medium-high heat, turning frequently, for 5 minutes, or until golden and crispy. Using a slotted spoon, transfer to a bowl. Add the chorizo to the pan and cook, stirring, for 1 minute, or until beginning to crisp. Add to the chicken.

• Heat another 3 tablespoons of the oil in the pan and cook the onions, stirring frequently, for 2 minutes, then add the garlic and paprika and cook, stirring, for an additional 3 minutes, or until the onions are soft but not browned.

• Add the drained rice, beans, and peas and stir until coated in oil. Return the chicken and chorizo and any accumulated juices to the pan. Stir in the stock, saffron and its soaking liquid, and salt and pepper to taste and bring to a boil, stirring constantly. Reduce the heat to low and let simmer, uncovered and without stirring, for 15 minutes, or until the rice is almost tender and most of the liquid has been absorbed.

• Arrange the mussels, shrimp, and red bell pepper slices on top, then cover and let simmer, without stirring, for an additional 5 minutes, or until the shrimp turn pink and the mussels open. Discard any mussels that remain closed. Taste and adjust the seasoning if necessary. Sprinkle with the parsley and serve immediately.

SERVES 4–6

½ tsp saffron threads

2 tbsp hot water

3 tbsp olive oil

6 oz/175 g Spanish chorizo sausage, casing removed, cut into ½-inch/ 1-cm slices

6 oz/175 g serrano ham, diced (if unavailable, use prosciutto)

1 large onion, chopped

2 garlic cloves, crushed

1 tsp paprika

¼ tsp cayenne pepper

8 oz/225 g tomatoes, peeled and cut into wedges

1 red bell pepper, halved and seeded, then broiled, peeled, and sliced

1⅝ cups medium-grain paella rice

1 tbsp chopped fresh thyme

generous ⅓ cup white wine

5 cups simmering beef or chicken stock or water

salt and pepper

1 tbsp chopped fresh parsley, to garnish

1 lemon, cut into wedges, to serve

Chorizo and Ham Paella

To add an extra flourish to the presentation, cook the lemon wedges on a hot grill pan or under a high broiler until well browned. Let stand until cool enough to handle before serving with the paella. As well as looking good, the wedges will yield lots of warm juice for squeezing over the dish.

• Put the saffron threads and water in a small bowl or cup and let infuse for a few minutes.

• Meanwhile, heat 2 tablespoons of the oil in a paella pan or wide, shallow skillet and cook the chorizo and ham over medium heat, stirring, for 5 minutes. Using a slotted spoon, transfer the meat to a bowl and set aside.

• Heat the remaining oil in the pan and cook the onion, stirring, for 2–3 minutes, or until softened. Add the garlic, paprika, cayenne pepper, and saffron and its soaking liquid and cook, stirring constantly, for 1 minute. Add the tomato wedges and red bell pepper slices and cook, stirring, for an additional 2 minutes.

• Add the rice and thyme and cook, stirring constantly, for 1 minute, or until the rice is glossy and coated. Pour in the wine and about 4 cups of the hot stock and bring to a boil. Reduce the heat and let simmer, uncovered, for 10 minutes. Do not stir during cooking, but shake the pan once or twice. Season to taste with salt and pepper, then shake the pan and cook for an additional 10 minutes, or until the rice grains are plump and almost cooked. If the liquid is absorbed too quickly, pour in a little more hot stock, then shake the pan to spread the liquid through the paella. Do not stir it in. Return the chorizo and ham and any accumulated juices to the pan, then add the red bell pepper and shake the pan, but do not stir. Cook for an additional 2 minutes.

• When all the liquid has been absorbed and you detect a faint toasty aroma coming from the rice, remove from the heat immediately to prevent burning. Cover the pan with a clean dish towel or foil and let stand for 5 minutes. Sprinkle over the parsley to garnish and serve direct from the pan with the lemon wedges for squeezing over the rice. Alternatively, divide the paella between warmed plates and garnish with the parsley, then serve with the lemon wedges.

SERVES 4–6

6 tbsp olive oil

3 tbsp sherry vinegar

¼ tsp cayenne pepper

1 tsp paprika

6 oz/175 g pork tenderloin

½ tsp saffron threads

2 tbsp hot water

2 large red bell peppers

6 oz/175 g Spanish chorizo sausage,
    casing removed, cut into ½-inch/
    1-cm slices

1 large onion, chopped

2 garlic cloves, crushed

8 oz/225 g tomatoes, peeled and cut
    into wedges

1⅝ cups medium-grain paella rice

1 tbsp chopped fresh thyme

generous ⅓ cup white wine

5 cups simmering beef or chicken
    stock or water

salt and pepper

1 lemon, cut into wedges, to serve

Paella with Pork and Chargrilled Peppers

This paella works very well if you omit the marinating stage. Simply cut the pork tenderloin into bite-size chunks and heat the marinade ingredients in the pan, then cook the pork for five minutes as directed in the third paragraph. Proceed with the recipe.

• Mix half the oil, vinegar, cayenne pepper, and paprika together in a shallow nonmetallic dish. Season the pork to taste with salt and pepper on both sides, then add to the oil mixture and turn in it until well coated. Cover with plastic wrap and let marinate in the refrigerator for 2 hours.

• Meanwhile, put the saffron threads and water in a small bowl or cup and let infuse for a few minutes. Preheat the broiler to high. Halve the bell peppers lengthwise, leaving the stems on to make removal of the cores and seeds easier, and flatten on the broiler rack, skin-side up. Cook under the broiler for 15 minutes, or until the skin is blackened and charred. Remove from the broiler, then transfer to a plastic bag and let stand for 15 minutes. Remove the skin, cores, and seeds and cut the flesh into long, thin strips about ½ inch/1 cm wide.

• Remove the pork from the marinade and cut into bite-size chunks. Heat the remaining oil in a paella pan or wide, shallow skillet and cook the pork and its marinade over medium heat, stirring, for 5 minutes. Add the chorizo and onion and cook, stirring, for 2–3 minutes, or until the onion is softened. Add the garlic and saffron and its soaking liquid and cook, stirring constantly, for 1 minute. Add the tomato wedges and cook, stirring, for an additional 2 minutes.

• Add the rice and thyme and cook, stirring constantly, for 1 minute, or until the rice is glossy and coated. Pour in the wine and about 4 cups of the hot stock and bring to a boil. Reduce the heat and let simmer, uncovered, for 10 minutes. Do not stir during cooking, but shake the pan once or twice. Season to taste with salt and pepper, then shake the pan and cook for an additional 10–15 minutes, or until the rice grains are plump and cooked. If the liquid is absorbed too quickly, pour in a little more hot stock, then shake the pan to spread the liquid through the paella. Do not stir it in.

• When all the liquid has been absorbed and you detect a faint toasty aroma coming from the rice, remove from the heat immediately to prevent burning. Cover the pan with a clean dish towel or foil and let stand for 5 minutes. Serve direct from the pan with the lemon wedges to squeeze over the rice. Alternatively, divide the paella between warmed plates and serve with the lemon wedges.

SERVES 4–6

1 tbsp butter

2 tbsp olive oil

1 red onion, chopped

¾ cup medium-grain paella rice

1 tsp turmeric

1 tsp ground cumin

½ tsp chili powder

3 garlic cloves, crushed

1 fresh green chili, sliced

1 green bell pepper, seeded
and diced

1 red bell pepper, seeded and diced

2¾ oz/75 g baby corn, halved
lengthwise

2 tbsp pitted black olives

1 large tomato, seeded and diced

2 cups vegetable stock

generous ½ cup unsalted
cashew nuts

scant ½ cup frozen peas

2 tbsp chopped fresh parsley,
plus extra sprigs to garnish

pinch of cayenne pepper

salt and pepper

Cashew Nut Paella

As a variation, try pine
nuts in place of the
cashew nuts, lightly
toasted beforehand in a
dry heavy-bottom skillet.

• Melt the butter with the oil in a paella pan or wide, shallow skillet and cook the onion over medium heat, stirring, for 2–3 minutes, or until softened.

• Add the rice, turmeric, cumin, chili powder, garlic, chili, bell peppers, baby corn, olives, and tomato and cook, stirring constantly, for 1–2 minutes. Pour in the stock and bring to a boil. Reduce the heat and cook, stirring frequently, for 20 minutes.

• Add the nuts and peas and cook, stirring occasionally, for 5 minutes. Season to taste with salt and pepper and sprinkle with the chopped parsley and cayenne pepper. Transfer to warmed serving plates, then garnish with parsley sprigs and serve immediately.

SERVES 4–6

½ tsp saffron threads

2 tbsp hot water

6 tbsp olive oil

1 Spanish onion, sliced

3 garlic cloves, minced

1 red bell pepper, seeded and sliced

1 orange bell pepper, seeded
   and sliced

1 large eggplant, cubed

1 cup medium-grain paella rice

2½ cups vegetable stock

1 lb/450 g tomatoes, peeled
   and chopped

4 oz/115 g mushrooms, sliced

4 oz/115 g green beans, halved

14 oz/400 g canned pinto beans

salt and pepper

Vegetarian Paella

You can use other kinds of canned beans instead of the pinto beans, such as cannellini or flageolets. Use drained canned Italian plum tomatoes if you cannot find sweet, ripe fresh tomatoes.

• Put the saffron threads and water in a small bowl or cup and let infuse for a few minutes.

• Meanwhile, heat the oil in a paella pan or wide, shallow skillet and cook the onion over medium heat, stirring, for 2–3 minutes, or until softened. Add the garlic, bell peppers, and eggplant and cook, stirring frequently, for 5 minutes.

• Add the rice and cook, stirring constantly, for 1 minute, or until glossy and coated. Pour in the stock and add the tomatoes, saffron and its soaking water, and salt and pepper to taste. Bring to a boil, then reduce the heat and let simmer, shaking the skillet frequently and stirring occasionally, for 15 minutes.

• Stir in the mushrooms, green beans, and pinto beans with their can juices. Cook for an additional 10 minutes, then serve immediately.

SERVES 4–6

½ tsp saffron threads

2 tbsp hot water

3 tbsp olive oil

1 large onion, chopped

1 zucchini, coarsely chopped

2 garlic cloves, crushed

¼ tsp cayenne pepper

8 oz/225 g tomatoes, peeled and cut
  into wedges

15 oz/425 g canned chickpeas,
  drained

15 oz/425 g canned artichokes hearts,
  drained and coarsely sliced

1⅝ cups medium-grain paella rice

5½ cups simmering vegetable stock

5½ oz/150 g green beans, blanched

salt and pepper

1 lemon, cut into wedges, to serve

Artichoke Paella

To ensure that your paella cooks evenly, turn the pan around now and then to make sure that every part of it has its share of the heat. Better still, cook it over two stove rings. This is possible if you have a very large paella pan, but if you don't, just keep moving the pan around one stove ring.

• Put the saffron threads and water in a small bowl or cup and let infuse for a few minutes.

• Meanwhile, heat the oil in a paella pan or wide, shallow skillet and cook the onion and zucchini over medium heat, stirring, for 2–3 minutes, or until softened. Add the garlic, cayenne pepper, and saffron and its soaking liquid and cook, stirring constantly, for 1 minute. Add the tomato wedges, chickpeas, and artichokes and cook, stirring, for an additional 2 minutes.

• Add the rice and cook, stirring constantly, for 1 minute, or until the rice is glossy and coated. Pour in about 5 cups of the hot stock and bring to a boil. Reduce the heat and let simmer, uncovered, for 10 minutes. Do not stir during cooking, but shake the pan once or twice. Add the green beans and season to taste with salt and pepper. Shake the pan and cook for an additional 10–15 minutes, or until the rice grains are plump and cooked. If the liquid is absorbed too quickly, pour in a little more hot stock, then shake the pan to spread the liquid through the paella. Do not stir it in.

• When all the liquid has been absorbed and you detect a faint toasty aroma coming from the rice, remove from the heat immediately to prevent burning. Cover the pan with a clean dish towel or foil and let stand for 5 minutes. Serve direct from the pan with the lemon wedges to squeeze over the rice. Alternatively, divide the paella between warmed plates and serve with the lemon wedges.

SERVES 4–6

½ tsp saffron threads

2 tbsp hot water

3 tbsp olive oil

1 large onion, chopped

2 garlic cloves, crushed

1 tsp paprika

8 oz/225 g tomatoes, peeled and
cut into wedges

1 red bell pepper, halved and seeded,
then broiled, peeled, and sliced

1 green bell pepper, halved and
seeded, then broiled, peeled,
and sliced

15 oz/425 g canned chickpeas,
drained

1⅝ cups medium-grain paella rice

5½ cups simmering vegetable stock

⅜ cup shelled peas

5½ oz/150 g fresh asparagus spears,
blanched

1 tbsp chopped fresh flat-leaf parsley,
plus extra to garnish

salt and pepper

1 lemon, cut into wedges, to serve

Paella de Verduras

This is an excellent paella for vegetarians and vegans, and anyone who has an intolerance to dairy products. For best results, use your own fresh, homemade vegetable stock (if your tap water has a strong smell or taste of chlorine, use filtered or mineral water in order to keep the taste of chlorine out of your paella). However, the paella also works well with commercially prepared stock—choose a good-quality variety without too much salt.

• Put the saffron threads and water in a small bowl or cup and let infuse for a few minutes.

• Meanwhile, heat the oil in a paella pan or wide, shallow skillet and cook the onion over medium heat, stirring, for 2–3 minutes, or until softened. Add the garlic, paprika, and saffron and its soaking liquid and cook, stirring constantly, for 1 minute. Add the tomato wedges, bell pepper slices, and chickpeas and cook, stirring, for an additional 2 minutes.

• Add the rice and cook, stirring constantly, for 1 minute, or until glossy and coated. Pour in about 5 cups of the hot stock and bring to a boil. Reduce the heat and let simmer, uncovered, for 10 minutes. Do not stir during cooking, but shake the pan once or twice. Add the peas, asparagus, and parsley and season to taste with salt and pepper. Shake the pan and cook for an additional 10–15 minutes, or until the rice grains are plump and cooked. If the liquid is absorbed too quickly, pour in a little more hot stock, then shake the pan to spread the liquid through the paella. Do not stir it in.

• When all the liquid has been absorbed and you detect a faint toasty aroma coming from the rice, remove from the heat immediately to prevent burning. Cover the pan with a clean dish towel or foil and let stand for 5 minutes. Sprinkle over chopped parsley to garnish and serve direct from the pan with the lemon wedges for squeezing over the rice. Alternatively, divide the paella between warmed plates and garnish with the parsley, then serve with the lemon wedges.

SERVES 4–6

½ tsp saffron threads

2 tbsp hot water

3 tbsp olive oil

1 large red onion, minced

2 garlic cloves, crushed

1 small fresh red chili, seeded and minced

1 tsp paprika

¼ tsp cayenne pepper

1 red bell pepper, halved and seeded, then broiled, peeled, and sliced

8 oz/225 g tomatoes, peeled and cut into wedges

6 oz/175 g canned chickpeas (drained weight)

6 oz/175 g canned red kidney beans (drained weight)

6 oz/175 g canned lima beans (drained weight)

1⅝ cups medium-grain paella rice

5½ cups hot vegetable stock

5½ oz/150 g green beans, blanched

salt and pepper

1 tbsp chopped fresh flat-leaf parsley, plus extra to garnish

1 lemon, cut into wedges, to serve

Spicy Three-Bean Paella

This is a highly nutritious paella for vegetarians and vegans because it is rich in protein. Try ringing the changes by experimenting with different combinations of beans. For example, you could try fava beans, black-eye peas, or adzuki beans.

You can also vary the amount and combination of spices to give different levels of heat intensity. If you prefer a milder heat, leave out the chili and halve the amount of cayenne pepper.

• Put the saffron threads and water in a small bowl or cup and let infuse for a few minutes.

• Meanwhile, heat the oil in a paella pan or wide, shallow skillet and cook the onion over medium heat, stirring, for 2–3 minutes, or until softened. Add the garlic, chili, paprika, cayenne pepper, and saffron and its soaking liquid and cook, stirring constantly, for 1 minute. Add the red bell pepper slices, tomato wedges, chickpeas, kidney beans, and lima beans and cook, stirring, for an additional 2 minutes.

• Add the rice and cook, stirring constantly, for 1 minute, or until glossy and coated. Pour in about 5 cups of the hot stock and bring to a boil. Reduce the heat and let simmer, uncovered, for 10 minutes. Do not stir during cooking, but shake the pan once or twice. Add the green beans and the parsley and season to taste with salt and pepper. Shake the pan and cook for 10–15 minutes, or until the rice grains are plump and cooked. If the liquid is absorbed too quickly, pour in a little more hot stock, then shake the pan to spread the liquid through the paella. Do not stir it in.

• When all the liquid has been absorbed and you detect a faint toasty aroma coming from the rice, remove from the heat immediately to prevent burning. Cover the pan with a clean dish towel or foil and let stand for 5 minutes. Sprinkle over chopped parsley to garnish and serve direct from the pan with the lemon wedges for squeezing over the rice. Alternatively, divide the paella between warmed plates and garnish with the parsley, then serve with the lemon wedges.

SERVES 4–6

½ tsp saffron threads

2 tbsp hot water

4 tbsp olive oil

1 large carrot, blanched and minced

1 large onion, chopped

2 garlic cloves, crushed

1 tsp paprika

¼ tsp cayenne pepper

8 oz/225 g tomatoes, peeled and
cut into wedges

1 red bell pepper, halved and seeded,
then broiled, peeled, and sliced

1⅝ cups medium-grain paella rice

1 tbsp chopped fresh thyme

5½ cups simmering chicken stock
or water

6 oz/175 g cooked pork, cut into
bite-size pieces

6 oz/175 g cooked chicken, cut into
bite-size pieces

5½ oz/150 g green beans, blanched,
or the same quantity of any
leftover cooked vegetables

3 hard-cooked eggs, cut lengthwise
into fourths

salt and pepper

1 lemon, cut into wedges, to serve

Poor Man's Paella

Poor man's paella is a delicious way to use up any leftover meat and vegetables. You can experiment with many different combinations. For example, try using your leftover Christmas turkey, or traditional roast beef. Simply replace the pork and chicken in this recipe with the same quantity of whatever cooked meat you have to hand. You can also use chicken-flavored mycoprotein to create a vegetarian version.

• Put the saffron threads and water in a small bowl or cup and let infuse for a few minutes.

• Meanwhile, heat half the oil in a paella pan or wide, shallow skillet and cook the carrot over medium heat, stirring, for 3 minutes. Add the onion and cook, stirring, for 2 minutes, or until softened. Add half the garlic, the paprika, cayenne pepper, and saffron and its soaking liquid and cook, stirring constantly, for 1 minute. Add the tomato wedges and red bell pepper slices and cook, stirring, for an additional 2 minutes.

• Add the rice and thyme and cook, stirring constantly, for 1 minute, or until the rice is glossy and coated. Pour in about 5 cups of the hot stock and bring to a boil. Reduce the heat and let simmer, uncovered, for 10 minutes. Do not stir during cooking, but shake the pan once or twice.

• Meanwhile, heat the remaining oil in a separate skillet and cook the remaining garlic, pork, and chicken over high heat, stirring, for 5 minutes. The heat should be high enough for the meat to become hot and steamy (leftover cooked meat and poultry should be reheated to a temperature of at least 167°F/75°C all the way through in order to kill off any potentially harmful bacteria).

• Transfer the meat mixture to the paella pan, then add the beans and season to taste with salt and pepper. Shake the pan and cook for an additional 10–15 minutes, or until the rice grains are plump and cooked. If the liquid is absorbed too quickly, pour in a little more hot stock, then shake the pan to spread the liquid through the paella. Do not stir it in.

• When all the liquid has been absorbed and you detect a faint toasty aroma coming from the rice, remove from the heat immediately to prevent burning. Cover the pan with a clean dish towel or foil and let stand for 5 minutes. Garnish with the egg quarters and serve direct from the pan with the lemon wedges for squeezing over the rice. Alternatively, divide the paella between warmed plates and garnish with the egg quarters, then serve with the lemon wedges.

The paellas in this chapter are truly inspirational, with some delicious interpretations of traditional paellas, such as the rich Paella Valenciana, with game and fresh rosemary, and some exciting innovations, such as Paella-Stuffed Mediterranean Peppers—juicy red bell peppers filled with a flavorful combination of rice, beans, vegetables, and Spanish manchego cheese, baked in the oven until tender.

The Outdoor Paella in this chapter, which is cooked on the grill, is the perfect dish to share with friends. Men, in particular, love to cook alfresco, and it is no coincidence that outdoor paellas in Spain are often cooked by the man of the house. Children also enjoy helping to prepare the ingredients, so cooking a paella is a great way for the whole family to get together.

EXTRA SPECIAL

One of the main ways of ensuring a flavor-filled paella is to sauté almost all the ingredients before you pour in the stock or water. Do not be tempted to boil the rice, because this will spoil the result. Although most of the ingredients in paellas are cooked in oil, only a very little is used, resulting in a healthy, nutritious dish, particularly as they contain a variety of fresh vegetables and beans. And since they are cooked and eaten in one large pan, with only a pan of simmering stock on the side, cleaning the pans is kept to a minimum!

SERVES 4–6

½ tsp saffron threads

2 tbsp hot water

3 tbsp olive oil

6 oz/175 g serrano ham, diced
(if unavailable, use prosciutto)

1 large carrot, diced

5½ oz/150 g white mushrooms

4 large scallions, diced

2 garlic cloves, crushed

1 tsp paprika

¼ tsp cayenne pepper

8 oz/225 g tomatoes, peeled and cut
into wedges

1 red bell pepper, halved and seeded,
then broiled, peeled, and sliced

1 green bell pepper, halved and
seeded, then broiled, peeled,
and sliced

1⅝ cups medium-grain paella rice

2 tbsp chopped mixed fresh herbs,
plus extra to garnish

generous ⅓ cup white wine

5 cups simmering beef or chicken
stock or water

⅜ cup shelled peas

3½ oz/100 g fresh asparagus spears,
blanched

salt and pepper

1 lemon, cut into wedges, to serve

Paella Primavera

Primavera means "spring" in Spanish, and you can experiment by using different seasonal spring vegetables in this paella. You can also replace the white mushrooms with the same quantity of wild mushrooms, such as cépe, shiitake, or morel, or a combination of them.

• Put the saffron threads and water in a small bowl or cup and let infuse for a few minutes.

• Meanwhile, heat 2 tablespoons of the oil in a paella pan or wide, shallow skillet and cook the ham over medium heat, stirring, for 5 minutes.

• Using a slotted spoon, transfer the ham to a bowl and set aside. Heat the remaining oil in the pan and cook the carrot, stirring, for 3 minutes. Add the mushrooms and cook, stirring, for 2 minutes. Add the scallions, garlic, paprika, cayenne pepper, and saffron and its soaking liquid and cook, stirring constantly, for 1 minute. Add the tomato wedges and bell pepper slices and cook, stirring, for an additional 2 minutes.

• Add the rice and herbs and cook, stirring constantly, for 1 minute, or until the rice is glossy and coated. Pour in the wine and about 4 cups of the hot stock and bring to a boil. Reduce the heat and let simmer, uncovered, for 10 minutes. Do not stir during cooking, but shake the pan once or twice. Add the peas and season to taste with salt and pepper. Shake the pan and cook for an additional 10 minutes, or until the rice grains are plump and almost cooked. If the liquid is absorbed too quickly, pour in a little more hot stock, then shake the pan to spread the liquid through the paella. Do not stir it in. Return the ham and any accumulated juices to the pan and shake the pan, but do not stir. Arrange the asparagus around the paella in a wheel pattern and cook for an additional 2 minutes.

• When all the liquid has been absorbed and you detect a faint toasty aroma coming from the rice, remove from the heat immediately to prevent burning. Cover the pan with a clean dish towel or foil and let stand for 5 minutes. Sprinkle over chopped herbs to garnish and serve direct from the pan with the lemon wedges for squeezing over the rice. Alternatively, divide the paella between warmed plates and garnish with the herbs, then serve with the lemon wedges.

SERVES 4–6

½ tsp saffron threads

2 tbsp hot water

3 tbsp olive oil

2 red onions, chopped

2 garlic cloves, crushed

1 tsp paprika

8 oz/225 g tomatoes, peeled and cut into wedges

1 red bell pepper, halved and seeded, then broiled, peeled, and sliced

15 oz/425 g canned lima beans, drained

1⅝ cups medium-grain paella rice

5½ cups simmering vegetable stock

⅜ cup shelled peas

⅜ cup corn kernels

20 black olives, pitted and halved (optional)

1 tbsp chopped fresh flat-leaf parsley

1 tbsp chopped fresh thyme

3½ oz/100 g Spanish manchego cheese

salt and pepper

1 lemon, cut into wedges, to serve

Lima Bean and Manchego Paella

Manchego is a famous Spanish cheese, with a full flavor and a firm texture that melts beautifully. However, if it is unavailable you can replace it with the same quantity of fresh Parmesan cheese shavings. Although Parmesan is Italian rather than Spanish, its flavor and texture work very well in this dish.

• Put the saffron threads and water in a small bowl or cup and let infuse for a few minutes.

• Meanwhile, heat the oil in a paella pan or wide, shallow skillet and cook the onions over medium heat, stirring, for 2–3 minutes, or until softened. Add the garlic, paprika, and saffron and its soaking liquid and cook, stirring constantly, for 1 minute. Add the tomato wedges, bell pepper slices, and lima beans and cook, stirring, for an additional 2 minutes.

• Add the rice and cook, stirring constantly, for 1 minute, or until glossy and coated. Pour in about 5 cups of the hot stock and bring to a boil. Reduce the heat and let simmer, uncovered, for 10 minutes. Do not stir during cooking, but shake the pan once or twice. Add the peas, corn, olives, if using, and herbs and season to taste with salt and pepper. Shake the pan and cook for an additional 10–15 minutes, or until the rice grains are plump and cooked. If the liquid is absorbed too quickly, pour in a little more hot stock, then shake the pan to spread the liquid through the paella. Do not stir it in.

• When all the liquid has been absorbed and you detect a faint toasty aroma coming from the rice, remove from the heat immediately to prevent burning. Cover the pan with a clean dish towel or foil and let stand for 5 minutes.

• Meanwhile, use a potato peeler to shave the cheese. Sprinkle the cheese shavings over the paella and serve direct from the pan with the lemon wedges for squeezing over the rice. Alternatively, divide the paella between warmed plates, and sprinkle over the cheese shavings, then serve with the lemon wedges.

SERVES 4

½ tsp saffron threads

2 tbsp hot water

3 tbsp olive oil

1 zucchini, diced

5½ oz/150 g white mushrooms

2 scallions, diced

2 garlic cloves, crushed

1 tsp paprika

¼ tsp cayenne pepper

9 oz/250 g canned red kidney beans
(drained weight)

8 oz/225 g tomatoes, peeled and
chopped

1⅝ cups medium-grain paella rice

5½ cups simmering vegetable stock

⅜ cup shelled peas

1 tbsp chopped fresh flat-leaf parsley,
plus extra to garnish

4 large red bell peppers

3½ oz/100 g manchego cheese or
Parmesan cheese, grated

salt and pepper

TO SERVE

mixed salad

warm crusty bread

Paella-Stuffed Mediterranean Peppers

This recipe is suitable for vegetarians and vegans. For meat eaters, cook 5½ oz/150 g diced serrano ham, or prosciutto, in 1 tablespoon olive oil for 5 minutes, then mix it with the paella just before stuffing the bell peppers.

If you are cooking for vegetarians and meat-eaters at the same time, divide the paella in half, then mix the cooked ham into one half and use it to fill two of the bell peppers, and fill the remaining two bell peppers with the meatless half of the paella.

• Put the saffron threads and water in a small bowl or cup and let infuse for a few minutes.

• Meanwhile, heat the oil in a paella pan or wide, shallow skillet and cook the zucchini over medium heat, stirring, for 3 minutes. Add the mushrooms and scallions and cook, stirring, for 2–3 minutes, or until softened. Add the garlic, paprika, cayenne pepper, and saffron and its soaking liquid and cook, stirring constantly, for 1 minute. Add the beans and chopped tomatoes and cook, stirring, for an additional 2 minutes.

• Add the rice and cook, stirring constantly, for 1 minute, or until glossy and coated. Pour in the wine and about 5 cups of the hot stock and bring to a boil. Reduce the heat and let simmer, uncovered, for 10 minutes. Do not stir during cooking, but shake the pan once or twice. Add the peas and parsley and season to taste with salt and pepper. Shake the pan and cook for an additional 10–15 minutes, or until the rice grains are plump and cooked. If the liquid is absorbed too quickly, pour in a little more hot stock, then shake the pan to spread the liquid through the paella. Do not stir it in.

• When all the liquid has been absorbed and you detect a faint toasty aroma coming from the rice, remove from the heat immediately to prevent burning. Cover the pan with a clean dish towel or foil and let stand for 5 minutes.

• Meanwhile, preheat the oven to 350°F/180°C. Cut the tops off the red bell peppers and remove the seeds, then blanch the bell peppers and their tops in a pan of boiling water for 2 minutes. Drain and let cool for a few seconds in cold water, then drain again and pat dry with paper towels. Spoon a little cheese into each bell pepper, then fill with paella and top with the remaining cheese. Replace the tops. Wrap each bell pepper in foil, then stand upright in an ovenproof dish and bake in the preheated oven for 25–30 minutes.

• Garnish with chopped parsley and serve with a mixed salad and warm crusty bread.

SERVES 4–6

5¼ cups fish stock or water

12 large raw shrimp, in their shells

½ tsp saffron threads

2 tbsp hot water

3½ oz/100 g skinless, boneless chicken breast, cut into ½-inch/1-cm pieces

3½ oz/100 g pork tenderloin, cut into ½-inch/1-cm pieces

3 tbsp olive oil

3½ oz/100 g Spanish chorizo sausage, casing removed, cut into ½-inch/1-cm slices

1 large red onion, chopped

2 garlic cloves, crushed

½ tsp cayenne pepper

½ tsp paprika

1 red bell pepper, seeded and sliced

1 green bell pepper, seeded and sliced

12 cherry tomatoes, halved

1⅝ cups medium-grain paella rice

1 tbsp chopped fresh parsley

2 tsp chopped fresh tarragon

salt and pepper

1 lemon and 1 lime, cut into wedges, to serve

Outdoor Paella

You can garnish this paella with fresh tarragon sprigs, to add an extra boost of flavor, but use sparingly, as the herb has a strong flavor that can be overpowering in larger quantities. This recipe also works well with chopped fresh rosemary in place of the tarragon.

• Preheat or light a grill. Put the stock in a large pan and bring to a simmer on the grill. Add the shrimp and cook for 2 minutes. Using a slotted spoon, transfer to a bowl and set aside. Let the stock simmer. Put the saffron threads and water in a small bowl or cup and let infuse for a few minutes.

• Season the chicken and pork to taste with salt and pepper. Heat the oil in a paella pan or wide, shallow skillet and cook the chicken, pork, and chorizo over medium heat, stirring, for 5 minutes, or until golden. Add the onion and cook, stirring, for 2–3 minutes, or until softened. Add the garlic, cayenne pepper, paprika, and saffron and its soaking liquid and cook, stirring constantly, for 1 minute. Add the bell pepper slices and tomato halves and cook, stirring, for an additional 2 minutes.

• Add the rice and herbs and cook, stirring constantly, for 1 minute, or until the rice is glossy and coated. Pour in about 5 cups of the hot stock and bring to a boil. Reduce the heat and let simmer, uncovered, for 10 minutes. Do not stir during cooking, but shake the pan once or twice. Season to taste with salt and pepper, then shake the pan and cook for an additional 10 minutes, or until the rice grains are plump and almost cooked. If the liquid is absorbed too quickly, pour in a little more hot stock, then shake the pan to spread the liquid through the paella. Do not stir it in. Add the shrimp and shake the pan, but do not stir. Cook for an additional 2 minutes.

• When all the liquid has been absorbed and you detect a faint toasty aroma coming from the rice, remove from the heat immediately to prevent burning. Cover the pan with a clean dish towel or foil and let stand for 5 minutes. Serve direct from the pan with the lemon and lime wedges for squeezing over the rice. Alternatively, divide the paella between warmed plates and serve with the lemon and lime wedges.

SERVES 4–6

7 oz/200 g live mussels

½ tsp saffron threads

2 tbsp hot water

5½ oz/150 g cod fillet, skinned

5½ cups simmering fish stock
or water

12 large raw shrimp, shelled
and deveined

3 tbsp olive oil

5½ oz/150 g skinless, boneless
chicken breast, cut into
bite-size chunks

1 large red onion, chopped

2 garlic cloves, crushed

½ tsp cayenne pepper

½ tsp paprika

8 oz/225 g tomatoes, peeled and
cut into wedges

1 red bell pepper and 1 yellow bell
pepper, seeded and sliced

1⅝ cups medium-grain paella rice

scant 1 cup canned corn kernels,
drained

3 hard-cooked eggs, cut lengthwise
into fourths

salt and pepper

1 lemon, cut into wedges, to serve

Sunshine Paella

In addition to saffron, Spanish cooks often use a powdered coloring agent to give their paellas a lovely golden color. If you would like to intensify the golden color without using an artificial coloring agent, add ½ teaspoon turmeric along with the other spices.

• Soak the mussels in lightly salted water for 10 minutes. Put the saffron threads and water in a small bowl or cup and let infuse.

• Meanwhile, rinse the cod under cold running water, then add it to the pan of simmering stock and cook for 5 minutes. Using a slotted spoon, transfer the cod to a colander. Rinse under cold running water and drain. Add the shrimp to the stock and cook for 2 minutes. Meanwhile, cut the cod into chunks, then transfer to a bowl with the shrimp and set aside. Let the stock simmer.

• Clean the mussels by scrubbing or scraping the shells and pulling out any beards that are attached to them. Discard any with broken shells or any that refuse to close when tapped. Add the mussels to the stock and cook for 5 minutes, or until opened. Using a slotted spoon, transfer the mussels to the bowl with the other seafood, discarding any mussels that remain closed.

• Heat the oil in a paella pan or wide, shallow skillet. Season the chicken to taste with salt and pepper and cook over medium heat, stirring, for 5 minutes. Add the onion and cook, stirring, for 2–3 minutes, or until softened. Add the garlic, cayenne pepper, paprika, and saffron and its soaking liquid and cook, stirring constantly, for 1 minute. Add the tomato wedges and bell pepper slices and cook, stirring, for an additional 2 minutes.

• Add the rice and cook, stirring constantly, for 1 minute, or until glossy and coated. Pour in about 5 cups of the hot stock and bring to a boil. Reduce the heat and let simmer, uncovered, for 10 minutes. Do not stir during cooking, but shake the pan once or twice. Season to taste with salt and pepper, then shake the pan and cook for an additional 10 minutes, or until the rice grains are plump and almost cooked. If the liquid is absorbed too quickly, pour in a little more hot stock, then shake the pan to spread the liquid through the paella. Do not stir it in. Add the cod, shrimp, mussels, and corn and shake the pan, but do not stir. Cook for an additional 3 minutes.

• When all the liquid has been absorbed and you detect a faint toasty aroma coming from the rice, remove from the heat immediately. Arrange the egg quarters on the paella, then cover the pan with a clean dish towel or foil and let stand for 5 minutes. Divide the paella between warmed plates and serve with the lemon wedges.

SERVES 4–6

6 tbsp olive oil

3 tbsp sherry vinegar

1 tsp paprika

6 oz/175 g boneless rabbit, cut
into bite-size chunks

½ tsp saffron threads

2 tbsp hot water

4 large duck breasts, skinned and
cut into bite-size chunks

1 large onion, chopped

2 garlic cloves, crushed

8 oz/225 g tomatoes, peeled and
cut into wedges

1⅝ cups medium-grain paella rice

1 tbsp chopped fresh rosemary,
plus extra sprigs to garnish

generous ⅓ cup white wine

5 cups simmering chicken stock
or water

7 oz/200 g green beans, blanched

salt and pepper

1 lemon, cut into wedges, to serve

Paella Valenciana

Valencian cooks often disagree about which ingredients make up the authentic paella, but often you will see rabbit, duck, tomatoes, and green beans listed in the ingredients, and sometimes chicken. Snails are also popular. To incorporate snails here, simply add 5½ oz/150 g fresh or frozen cleaned snails along with the tomatoes. If you prefer not to use them, rosemary is an accepted alternative, as used in this recipe.

• Mix half the oil, vinegar, and paprika together in a shallow nonmetallic dish. Season the rabbit to taste with salt and pepper on both sides, then add to the oil mixture and turn in it until well coated. Cover with plastic wrap and let marinate in the refrigerator for 2 hours.

• Meanwhile, put the saffron threads and water in a bowl or cup and let infuse for a few minutes. Heat 1 teaspoon of the remaining oil in a large paella pan or wide, shallow skillet and cook the duck over medium-high heat, stirring, for 5 minutes, or until golden all over. Using a slotted spoon, transfer the duck to a bowl and set aside.

• Heat the remaining oil in the paella pan and cook the rabbit and its marinade over medium heat, stirring, for 5 minutes. Add the onion and cook, stirring, for 2–3 minutes, or until softened. Add the garlic and saffron and its soaking liquid and cook, stirring constantly, for 1 minute. Add the tomato wedges and cook, stirring, for an additional 2 minutes.

• Add the rice and rosemary and cook, stirring constantly, for 1 minute, or until the rice is glossy and coated. Pour in the wine and about 4 cups of the hot stock and bring to a boil. Reduce the heat and let simmer, uncovered, for 10 minutes. Do not stir during cooking, but shake the pan once or twice. Return the duck and any accumulated juices to the pan, then add the beans and season to taste with salt and pepper. Shake the pan and cook for an additional 10–15 minutes, or until the rice grains are plump and cooked. If the liquid is absorbed too quickly, pour in a little more hot stock, then shake the pan to spread the liquid through the paella. Do not stir it in.

• When all the liquid has been absorbed and you detect a faint toasty aroma coming from the rice, remove from the heat immediately to prevent burning. Cover the pan with a clean dish towel or foil and let stand for 5 minutes. Garnish with the rosemary sprigs and serve direct from the pan with the lemon wedges to squeeze over the rice. Alternatively, divide the paella between warmed plates and garnish with the rosemary, then serve with the lemon wedges.

SERVES 4–6

7 oz/200 g live mussels

½ tsp saffron threads

2 tbsp hot water

5½ oz/150 g cod fillet, skinned

5½ cups simmering fish stock
    or water

3 tbsp olive oil

1 large red onion, chopped

2 garlic cloves, crushed

½ tsp cayenne pepper

8 oz/225 g tomatoes, peeled and cut
    into wedges

1 red bell pepper, seeded and sliced

1 green bell pepper, seeded
    and sliced

1⅝ cups medium-grain paella rice

generous ⅓ cup white wine

1⅛ cup shelled peas

1 tbsp chopped fresh dill,
    plus extra to garnish

salt and pepper

1 lemon, cut into wedges, to serve

Paella with Mussels and White Wine

You can ring the changes
with the vegetables
by replacing the peas
with 5½ oz/150 g blanched
fresh asparagus spears or
blanched carrots cut into
thin sticks. Simply
add them with the dill
and omit the peas.

• Soak the mussels in lightly salted water for 10 minutes. Put the saffron threads and water in a small bowl or cup and let infuse.

• Meanwhile, rinse the cod under cold running water, then add it to the pan of simmering stock and cook for 5 minutes. Using a slotted spoon, transfer the cod to a colander. Rinse under cold running water and drain. Cut into chunks, then transfer to a bowl and set aside. Let the stock simmer.

• Clean the mussels by scrubbing or scraping the shells and pulling out any beards that are attached to them. Discard any with broken shells or any that refuse to close when tapped. Add the mussels to the stock and cook for 5 minutes, or until opened. Using a slotted spoon, transfer the mussels to the bowl with the cod, discarding any mussels that remain closed.

• Heat the oil in a paella pan or wide, shallow skillet and cook the onion over medium heat, stirring, for 2–3 minutes, or until softened. Add the garlic, cayenne pepper, and saffron and its soaking liquid and cook, stirring constantly, for 1 minute. Add the tomato wedges and bell pepper slices and cook, stirring, for an additional 2 minutes.

• Add the rice and cook, stirring constantly, for 1 minute, or until glossy and coated. Pour in the wine and about 4 cups of the hot stock and bring to a boil. Reduce the heat and let simmer, uncovered, for 10 minutes. Do not stir during cooking, but shake the pan once or twice. Add the peas and dill and season to taste with salt and pepper. Shake the pan and cook for an additional 10 minutes, or until the rice grains are plump and almost cooked. If the liquid is absorbed too quickly, pour in a little more hot stock, then shake the pan to spread the liquid through the paella. Do not stir it in. Add the cod and mussels and shake the pan, but do not stir. Cook for an additional 3 minutes.

• When all the liquid has been absorbed and you detect a faint toasty aroma coming from the rice, remove from the heat immediately to prevent burning. Cover the pan with a clean dish towel or foil and let stand for 5 minutes. Divide the paella between warmed plates and garnish with the dill, then serve with the lemon wedges.

SERVES 4–6

½ tsp saffron threads

2 tbsp hot water

6 oz/175 g skinless, boneless chicken breast, cut into bite-size chunks

4 large skinless, boneless duck breasts, cut into bite-size chunks

2 tbsp olive oil

1 large onion, chopped

2 garlic cloves, crushed

1 tsp paprika

8 oz/225 g tomatoes, peeled and cut into wedges

1 orange bell pepper, halved and seeded, then broiled, peeled, and coarsely chopped

6 oz/175 g canned red kidney beans (drained weight)

1⅝ cups medium-grain paella rice

1 tbsp chopped fresh flat-leaf parsley, plus extra sprigs to garnish

1 tbsp freshly grated orange rind

2 tbsp orange juice

generous ⅓ cup white wine

5 cups simmering chicken stock or water

salt and pepper

1 orange, cut into wedges, to serve

Chicken and Duck Paella with Orange

Duck and orange is a well-known and popular combination, but you could also use lemon in this dish. Simply replace the orange rind and juice with lemon rind and juice and serve with lemon wedges instead of orange wedges.

• Put the saffron threads and water in a small bowl or cup and let infuse for a few minutes.

• Meanwhile, season the chicken and duck to taste with salt and pepper. Heat the oil in a large paella pan or wide, shallow skillet and cook the chicken and duck over medium-high heat, stirring, for 5 minutes, or until golden all over. Using a slotted spoon, transfer the meat to a bowl and set aside.

• Add the onion and cook over medium heat, stirring, for 2–3 minutes, or until softened. Add the garlic, paprika, and saffron and its soaking liquid and cook, stirring constantly, for 1 minute. Add the tomato wedges, orange bell pepper, and beans and cook, stirring, for an additional 2 minutes.

• Add the rice and parsley and cook, stirring constantly, for 1 minute, or until the rice is glossy and coated. Add the orange rind and juice, wine, and about 4 cups of the hot stock and bring to a boil. Reduce the heat and let simmer, uncovered, for 10 minutes. Do not stir during cooking, but shake the pan once or twice. Return the chicken and duck and any accumulated juices to the pan and season to taste with salt and pepper. Shake the pan and cook for an additional 10–15 minutes, or until the rice grains are plump and cooked. If the liquid is absorbed too quickly, pour in a little more hot stock, then shake the pan to spread the liquid through the paella. Do not stir it in.

• When all the liquid has been absorbed and you detect a faint toasty aroma coming from the rice, remove from the heat immediately to prevent burning. Cover the pan with a clean dish towel or foil and let stand for 5 minutes. Garnish with parsley sprigs and serve direct from the pan with the orange wedges for squeezing over the rice. Alternatively, divide between warmed plates and garnish with the parsley, then serve with the orange wedges.

SERVES 4–6

½ tsp saffron threads

2 tbsp hot water

5½ oz/150 g pork tenderloin, cut into bite-size chunks

5½ oz/150 g skinless, boneless chicken breast, cut into bite-size chunks

1 tsp paprika

½ tsp cayenne pepper

3 tbsp olive oil

5½ oz/150 g Spanish chorizo sausage, casing removed, cut into ½-inch/1-cm slices

1 large red onion, chopped

2 garlic cloves, crushed

1 small fresh red chili, seeded and minced

8 oz/225 g cherry tomatoes, halved

1 red and 1 green bell pepper, halved and seeded, then broiled, peeled, and coarsely chopped

1⅝ cups medium-grain paella rice

1 tbsp chopped fresh thyme, plus extra sprigs to garnish

2 tbsp sherry

generous ⅓ cup white wine

5 cups simmering beef or chicken stock or water

12 black olives, pitted and halved

salt and pepper

1 lemon, cut into wedges, to serve

Fiery Chili and Chorizo Paella

Beef also works very well in this recipe. Simply replace the pork and chicken with 10½ oz/300 g lean beef, cut into bite-size chunks. Add along with the chorizo, and cook in the same way as the pork and chicken.

• Put the saffron threads and water in a small bowl or cup and let infuse for a few minutes.

• Meanwhile, season the pork and chicken with the paprika, cayenne pepper, and salt and pepper to taste. Heat the oil in a paella pan or wide, shallow skillet and cook the pork, chicken, and chorizo over medium heat, stirring, for 5 minutes. Add the onion and cook, stirring, for 2–3 minutes, or until softened. Add the garlic, chili, and saffron and its soaking liquid and cook, stirring constantly, for 1 minute. Add the tomatoes and bell peppers and cook, stirring, for an additional 2 minutes.

• Add the rice and thyme and cook, stirring constantly, for 1 minute, or until the rice is glossy and coated. Pour in the sherry, wine, and about 4 cups of the hot stock and bring to a boil. Reduce the heat and let simmer, uncovered, for 10 minutes. Do not stir during cooking, but shake the pan once or twice. Add the olives and season to taste with salt and pepper. Shake the pan and cook for an additional 10 minutes, or until the rice grains are plump and almost cooked. If the liquid is absorbed too quickly, pour in a little more hot stock, then shake the pan to spread the liquid through the paella. Do not stir it in. Taste and adjust the seasoning if necessary and cook for an additional 2 minutes.

• When all the liquid has been absorbed and you detect a faint toasty aroma coming from the rice, remove from the heat immediately to prevent burning. Cover the pan with a clean dish towel or foil and let stand for 5 minutes. Garnish with thyme sprigs and serve direct from the pan with the lemon wedges for squeezing over the rice. Alternatively, divide the paella between warmed plates and garnish with the thyme, then serve with the lemon wedges.

SERVES 4–6

½ tsp saffron threads

2 tbsp hot water

12 oz/350 g boneless lamb,
  cut into bite-size chunks

3 tbsp olive oil

5½ oz/150 g Spanish chorizo
  sausage, casing removed,
  cut into ½-inch/1-cm slices

4 shallots, chopped

2 garlic cloves, crushed

8 oz/225 g tomatoes, peeled and
  coarsely chopped

1 yellow bell pepper, halved and
  seeded, then broiled, peeled,
  and sliced

1⅝ cups medium-grain paella rice

1 tbsp chopped fresh rosemary, plus
  extra sprigs to garnish

generous ⅓ cup white wine

5 cups simmering beef or chicken
  stock or water

12 black olives, pitted and halved

5½ oz/150 g green beans, blanched

salt and pepper

1 lemon, cut into wedges, to serve

Lamb Paella with Rosemary

To add an extra kick to this recipe, before you start this dish, put the lamb chunks in a bowl with 3 tablespoons olive oil, 1 tablespoon sherry vinegar, 1 teaspoon paprika, and ½ teaspoon cayenne pepper. Cover with plastic wrap and let marinate in the refrigerator for 2 hours. Remove the lamb from the marinade and cook with the chorizo as directed in the recipe.

• Put the saffron threads and water in a small bowl or cup and let infuse for a few minutes.

• Meanwhile, season the lamb to taste with salt and pepper. Heat the oil in a paella pan or wide, shallow skillet and cook the lamb and chorizo over medium heat, stirring, for 5 minutes. Add the shallots and cook, stirring, for 2–3 minutes, or until softened. Add the garlic and saffron and its soaking liquid and cook, stirring constantly, for 1 minute. Add the tomatoes and yellow bell pepper slices and cook, stirring, for an additional 2 minutes.

• Add the rice and rosemary and cook, stirring constantly, for 1 minute, or until the rice is glossy and coated. Pour in the wine and about 4 cups of the hot stock and bring to a boil. Reduce the heat and let simmer, uncovered, for 10 minutes. Do not stir during cooking, but shake the pan once or twice. Add the olives and beans and season to taste with salt and pepper. Shake the pan and cook for an additional 10 minutes, or until the rice grains are plump and almost cooked. If the liquid is absorbed too quickly, pour in a little more hot stock, then shake the pan to spread the liquid through the paella. Do not stir it in. Taste and adjust the seasoning if necessary and cook for an additional 2 minutes.

• When all the liquid has been absorbed and you detect a faint toasty aroma coming from the rice, remove from the heat immediately to prevent burning. Cover the pan with a clean dish towel or foil and let stand for 5 minutes. Garnish with rosemary sprigs and serve direct from the pan with the lemon wedges for squeezing over the rice. Alternatively, divide the paella between warmed plates and garnish with the rosemary, then serve with the lemon wedges.

While paellas can be satisfying meals in themselves, there is nothing quite like some tasty tapas or appetizers, lovingly prepared, to whet the appetite in advance of the main event.

Tapas, which are Spanish in origin, are delicious morsels of food. The word *tapa* means "lid" and comes from the Spanish *tapar*, meaning "to cover." Like paella, there are a number of different stories relating to the origin of tapas, one of which is that bartenders in southern Spain began putting a slice of chorizo sausage or serrano ham on top of their customers' wine glasses to keep insects out. That led to the practice of serving little saucers of food, placed on the drink or alongside. Another story relates that tapas were originally invented by the army to stop the soldiers getting too drunk on their nights out, and yet another tells

TOTALLY TAPAS

that Castile's King Alfonso the Wise started the tapas tradition during his convalescence from an illness by drinking wine and eating small dishes between main meals. Whatever the origin of these delightful snacks, they have, like paella, become popular all round the world, and are constantly evolving, with exciting new interpretations being created all the time.

This chapter presents a tantalizing medley of tapas and appetizers, from piquant nibbles to quite substantial dishes. So, whichever paella you have chosen for the occasion, there is bound to be something here that will introduce it with a flourish.

SERVES 4–6

olive oil, for deep-frying

sweet or hot fresh green chilies

sea salt, for sprinkling

Deep-Fried Green Chilies

For a more elaborate tapa, top a thin slice of bread with a fried egg, yolk-side up. Secure the egg to the bread by skewering the set white to the bread with a toothpick, with a deep-fried chili threaded onto it.

• Heat a depth of 3 inches/7.5 cm oil in a heavy-bottom pan until it reaches 350–375°F/180–190°C, or until a cube of bread browns in 30 seconds.

• Rinse the chilies and pat thoroughly dry with paper towels. Drop into the hot oil and cook for no longer than 20 seconds, until they turn bright green and the skins blister.

• Remove with a slotted spoon and drain well on crumpled paper towels. Sprinkle with sea salt and serve immediately.

SERVES 4–6

1½ tbsp coarse sea salt

½ tsp smoked Spanish paprika
   or hot paprika, to taste

1 lb 2 oz/500 g blanched almonds

1 tbsp extra virgin olive oil

Paprika-Spiced Almonds

It is best, and more economical, to buy unblanched almonds and blanch them as and when required, because they begin to dry out as soon as the thin, brown skin is removed. Put the unblanched almonds in a heatproof bowl. Pour over boiling water and let stand for 1 minute. Drain well, then pat dry with paper towels and slip off the skins.

• Preheat the oven to 400°F/200°C. Put the sea salt and paprika in a mortar and grind to a fine powder with a pestle, or use a mini spice blender.

• Spread the almonds out on a cookie sheet and toast in the preheated oven, turning occasionally, for 8–10 minutes, or until golden brown and giving off a toasted aroma—watch carefully after 7 minutes because they quickly burn. Immediately tip into a heatproof bowl.

• Drizzle over the oil and stir to ensure that all the nuts are lightly and evenly coated. Add extra oil if necessary. Sprinkle with the salt and paprika mixture and stir again. Transfer to a small bowl and serve at room temperature.

SERVES 4–6

2 lb/900 g large, juicy tomatoes,
   halved

2 tbsp butter

1 tbsp olive oil

1 large onion, sliced

2–3 tbsp tomato paste, depending
   on the strength of flavor of the
   tomatoes

3½ cups vegetable stock

2 tbsp amontillado sherry

½ tsp sugar

salt and pepper

crusty bread, to serve

Rich Tomato Soup

If you don't possess a mouli, purée the soup in a blender or food processor, then work through a fine nylon strainer to achieve the smooth texture. You can also serve the soup chilled, swirling 1 tablespoon sour cream into each bowl and sprinkling with minced fresh parsley.

• Preheat the broiler to high. Place the tomatoes, cut-sides up, on a cookie sheet and cook under the broiler, about 4 inches/10 cm from the heat source, for 5 minutes, or until just beginning to char around the edges.

• Meanwhile, melt the butter with the oil in a large pan or ovenproof casserole and cook the onion over medium heat, stirring frequently, for 5 minutes. Stir in the tomato paste and cook for an additional 2 minutes.

• Add the tomatoes, stock, sherry, sugar, and salt and pepper to taste and stir well. Bring to a boil, then reduce the heat and let simmer, covered, for 20 minutes, or until the tomatoes are reduced to a pulp.

• Process the soup through a mouli into a large bowl. Return to the rinsed-out pan and let simmer, uncovered, for 10 minutes, or until the desired consistency is achieved. Ladle into individual bowls and serve with crusty bread.

MAKES 8–10 SLICES
½ cup olive oil
1 lb 5 oz/600 g potatoes, peeled
    and thinly sliced
1 large onion, thinly sliced

6 large eggs
salt and pepper
fresh flat-leaf parsley sprigs,
    to garnish

Spanish Tortilla

If you are not confident about inverting the tortilla, finish cooking it under a medium-high broiler, about 4 inches/10 cm from the heat source, until the runny egg mixture on top is set. The tortilla will not, however, have its characteristic "rounded" edge.

• Preheat a 10-inch/25-cm skillet, preferably nonstick, over high heat. Add the oil and heat. Reduce the heat and cook the potatoes and onion for 15–20 minutes, or until the potatoes are tender.

• Meanwhile, beat the eggs in a large bowl and season generously with salt and pepper. Drain the potatoes and onion through a strainer over a heatproof bowl to reserve the oil. Very gently stir the vegetables into the eggs, then set aside for 10 minutes.

• Use a wooden spoon or spatula to remove any crusty bits stuck to the bottom of the skillet. Reheat the skillet over medium-high heat with 4 tablespoons of the reserved oil. Add the egg mixture and smooth the surface, pressing the potatoes and onion into an even layer.

• Cook for 5 minutes, shaking the skillet occasionally, until the underside is set. Using a spatula, loosen the edge of the tortilla. Place a large plate over the top and carefully invert the skillet and plate together so that the tortilla drops onto the plate.

• Add 1 tablespoon of the remaining reserved oil to the skillet and swirl around. Carefully slide the tortilla back into the skillet, cooked-side up. Run the spatula around the tortilla, to tuck in the edge.

• Cook the tortilla for an additional 3 minutes, or until the eggs are set and the underside is golden brown. Remove from the heat and slide the tortilla onto a plate. Let stand for at least 5 minutes before cutting into slices. Serve warm or at room temperature, garnished with parsley sprigs.

SERVES 6

12 ripe figs

12 oz/350 g Spanish bleu cheese,
   such as Picós, crumbled

extra virgin olive oil, for drizzling

CARAMELIZED ALMONDS

½ cup superfine sugar

generous ¾ cup whole almonds,
   blanched or unblanched

butter, for greasing

Figs with Bleu Cheese

Store the nuts in an airtight jar for up to three days until required; any longer and they will become soft.

• First, make the Caramelized Almonds. Lightly grease a cookie sheet. Put the sugar in a pan and cook over medium-high heat, stirring, until melted and golden brown and bubbling. Do not stir once the mixture begins to bubble.

• Remove from the heat and add the almonds, one at a time, then quickly turn with a fork until well coated. If the caramel hardens, return the pan to the heat. Transfer each almond to the prepared cookie sheet once it is coated. Let stand until cool and firm.

• To serve, slice the figs in half and arrange 4 halves on each plate. Coarsely chop the almonds by hand. Arrange a mound of cheese on each plate and sprinkle with an equal quantity of the chopped almonds. Drizzle the figs very lightly with oil.

SERVES 4–6

4 tbsp olive oil

1 large garlic clove, halved

1 lb 2 oz/500 g small zucchini,
    thinly sliced

⅜ cup pine nuts

generous ⅓ cup raisins

3 tbsp minced fresh mint leaves
    (not spearmint or peppermint)

2 tbsp freshly squeezed lemon juice,
    or to taste

salt and pepper

Moorish Zucchini Salad

This salad is best made with young, tender zucchini no more than 1 inch/2.5 cm thick. If using older, larger zucchini, cut them in half or fourths lengthwise first, then thinly slice.

• Heat the oil in a large skillet and cook the garlic over medium heat until golden, to flavor the oil. Remove and discard the garlic. Add the zucchini and cook, stirring, until just tender. Using a slotted spoon, immediately remove from the skillet and transfer to a large serving bowl.
• Add the pine nuts, raisins, mint, lemon juice, and salt and pepper to taste to the bowl and stir well. Taste and add more oil, lemon juice, and salt and pepper if necessary.
• Set aside and let cool completely. Cover and let chill in the refrigerator for at least 3½ hours. Remove from the refrigerator 10 minutes before serving.

SERVES 6

60 large raw shrimp, thawed if frozen

2/3 cup olive oil

6 garlic cloves, thinly sliced

3 dried hot red chilies (optional)

6 tbsp freshly squeezed lemon juice

6 tbsp minced fresh parsley

French bread, to serve

Garlic Shrimp with Lemon and Parsley

To devein shrimp, use a fine-bladed knife to slice along the back from the head end to the tail, then remove the thin, black intestine.

• Remove the heads and shell and devein the shrimp, but leave the tails intact. Carefully pat the shrimp dry with paper towels.

• Heat the oil in a large, deep sauté pan or skillet and cook the garlic and chilies, if using, over medium-high heat, stirring, until they begin to sizzle. Add the shrimp and cook until they turn pink and curl.

• Using a slotted spoon, transfer the shrimp to warmed earthenware bowls. Sprinkle each bowl with a tablespoon of lemon juice and parsley. Serve immediately with plenty of bread to mop up the juices.

MAKES 16

16 pimientos del piquillo, drained, or
freshly roasted sweet peppers
(see below left), tops removed
chopped fresh parsley, to garnish

CRAB SALAD

1 red sweet pepper
8½ oz/240 g cooked fresh or
canned crabmeat, drained
and squeezed dry
about 2 tbsp freshly squeezed
lemon juice
scant 1 cup cream cheese
salt and pepper

Peppers Stuffed with Crab Salad

If you can't find pimientos del piquillo, and have to roast the peppers yourself, use 16 of the long, sweet Mediterranean variety, not the ordinary bell-shaped kind. If, however, the latter are the only ones you can find, cut 4–6 into wedges and spread the crab salad along each wedge.

• First, grill the red pepper. Preheat the broiler to high. Halve the pepper lengthwise, leaving the stem on to make removal of the core and seeds easier, and flatten on the broiler rack, skin-side up. Cook under the broiler for 15 minutes, or until the skin is blackened and charred. Remove from the broiler, then transfer to a plastic bag, and let stand for 15 minutes. Remove the skin, cores, and seeds. The broiled pepper will keep for up to 5 days in the refrigerator, covered with olive oil and wrapped in plastic wrap.

• Pick over the crabmeat and remove any bits of shell. Put half the crabmeat in a blender or food processor with the broiled red pepper, 1½ tablespoons of the lemon juice, and salt and pepper to taste. Process until well blended, then transfer to a bowl. Blend in the cream cheese and remaining crabmeat. Taste and add the extra lemon juice if required.

• Pat the pimientos del piquillo dry with paper towels and scoop out any seeds that remain in the tips. Use a small spoon to divide the crab salad equally between the peppers, stuffing them generously. Arrange on a large serving dish or individual plates, then cover and let chill until required. Just before serving, sprinkle the stuffed peppers with chopped parsley to garnish.

MAKES 12

12 slices French bread, diagonally
    sliced, about ¼ inch/5 mm thick
about 1½ oz/40 g cured, ready-to-eat
    chorizo sausage, cut into
    12 thin slices

olive oil, for pan-frying
12 quail's eggs
paprika, for sprinkling
salt and pepper

Chorizo and Quail's Eggs

Despite their delicate appearance, quail's eggs can be difficult to crack because of a relatively thick membrane under the shell. It is useful to have a pair of scissors handy to cut through the membrane as you break the eggs into the skillet.

• Preheat the broiler to high. Arrange the slices of bread on a cookie sheet and cook under the broiler until golden brown on both sides.

• Cut or fold the chorizo slices to fit on the toasts. Set aside.

• Heat a thin layer of oil in a large skillet over medium heat until a cube of day-old bread sizzles in 40 seconds. Break the eggs into the skillet and cook, spooning the fat over the yolks, until the whites are set and the yolks are cooked to your liking.

• Using a slotted spoon, remove the fried eggs from the skillet and drain on paper towels. Immediately transfer to the chorizo-topped toasts and dust with paprika. Sprinkle with salt and pepper to taste and serve immediately.

MAKES 12

12 anchovy fillets in oil, drained

24 pimiento-stuffed green olives in
   oil, drained

Olives Wrapped with Anchovies

Instead of using pimiento-stuffed olives, stuff pitted green or black olives with a blanched almond sliver. Proceed with the recipe as above.

• Thinly slice each anchovy fillet lengthwise. Wrap a half fillet around the middle of each olive, overlapping the ends, and secure with a wooden toothpick. Repeat with another olive and anchovy fillet half and slide onto the toothpick.

• Continue until all the ingredients are used up and you have 12 toothpicks with 2 anchovy-wrapped olives on each one.

If you still have room, what better way to round off a delicious paella than with a sumptuous Spanish dessert and a drink?

Vying for your attention in this chapter are the "Jeweled" Honey Mousses, made with thick heavy cream sweetened with honey and topped with the vibrant-colored seeds from pomegranates, and the Frozen Almond Cream with Hot Chocolate Sauce, which is pure indulgence itself. The Almond Tart also has a special allure, with its inspired pairing of sweet almonds and the citrus tang of orange. Since it is served cold, it will keep until whenever your guests are ready to it eat after the paella—it will go down a treat with a good cup of coffee. Or if the paella was substantial, serve the irresistible Dates Stuffed with Spanish Marzipan as a petit four.

DESSERTS AND DRINKS

The drinks are an additional delight. Sangria, which is made with full-flavored red wine, Spanish brandy, and ripe, tender fruits, is popular all over Spain, and has intoxicated many an unwary traveler! Hot Chocolate is another Spanish favorite. This thick, creamy, indulgent drink is full of mouthwatering melted chocolate with a hint of vanilla.

Rest assured that you will find something among these exciting concoctions to suit every occasion and palate. The only problem you are likely to encounter is how to satisfy all the people who are clamoring for more!

MAKES 12–14

12–14 dried dates

SPANISH MARZIPAN

⅝ cup confectioners' sugar, plus
extra for dusting

¾ cup ground almonds

¼ tsp almond extract

Dates Stuffed with Spanish Marzipan

You can vary the flavors of your Spanish marzipan according to your taste. For example, try adding 1 tablespoon finely grated orange or lemon rind, or minced candied fruit or minced pistachio to the basic recipe.

• To make the marzipan, sift the confectioners' sugar into a bowl and mix in the almonds. Sprinkle over the almond extract. Add a little water, $1/4$ teaspoon at a time, until the mixture comes together and can be pressed into a ball.

• Knead the marzipan with your hands and then on a counter lightly dusted with confectioners' sugar until it is smooth. It is now ready to be used, or can be wrapped in plastic wrap and stored in the refrigerator for up to 3 days.

• To stuff the dates, use a small knife to slice along the length of each, then open out and remove the pit. Break off a small piece of the marzipan and mold it into a "log," pressing it into a date. Repeat with the remaining dates and marzipan. Arrange the dates on a plate and serve with coffee after dinner.

SERVES 4–6

12 ripe apricots, halved and pitted

2 tbsp slivered almonds, toasted,
    to decorate

SYRUP

½ tsp fennel seeds

½ tsp coriander seeds

¼ tsp black peppercorns

1 cup superfine sugar

1 cup full-bodied Spanish red wine,
    such as Rioja

1 cup water

3 tbsp freshly squeezed orange juice

2 tbsp freshly squeezed lemon juice

2 tbsp Spanish cream sherry

3 cloves

1 cinnamon stick

Poached Fruit Seville-Style

Delicious desserts featuring ripe, juicy fruit and fragrant spices are typical of the Andalusian cuisine of southern Spain. In this recipe, apricots have been used, but you could just as easily use pears, apples, peaches, or nectarines. The fruit and syrup can be served on their own, or with vanilla ice cream.

• First, make the syrup. Preheat a heavy-bottom pan over high heat and dry-fry the fennel and coriander seeds and peppercorns for up to 1 minute, or until they start to give off an aroma. Immediately tip them out of the pan to prevent further cooking. Put in a mortar and lightly crush with a pestle.

• Put the remaining syrup ingredients in a heavy-bottom pan over medium-high heat and stir until the sugar has dissolved. Bring to a boil, without stirring, and let bubble for 5 minutes.

• Add the apricots and let simmer for 6–8 minutes, or until tender. Remove the pan from the heat, then transfer the apricots to a bowl of iced water and let cool. When cool enough to handle, remove the apricots and skin. Cover and let chill until required.

• Meanwhile, return the syrup mixture to the heat and boil until it thickens and the flavors become more concentrated. Remove from the heat and let cool.

• When ready to serve, arrange the fruit in serving bowls, then spoon over the syrup. Sprinkle with slivered almonds to decorate.

SERVES 6

3 cups milk

1 vanilla bean, split

thinly pared rind of ¼ lemon

7 large egg yolks

1 cup superfine sugar

3 tbsp cornstarch

Catalan Burned Cream

This classic Spanish dessert is not to be confused with the French crème brûlée. It is not baked like the French dish, so it remains runny. You need to prepare the custard at least 12 hours in advance, to enable it to thicken in the refrigerator. You can also make a spiced version of this dish by adding 1 teaspoon ground cinnamon with the lemon rind in the first paragraph.

• Prepare the custard a day in advance of serving. Put the milk into a pan with the vanilla bean and lemon rind and bring to a boil. Remove from the heat and let stand for at least 30 minutes to infuse.

• Put the eggs and ½ cup of the sugar in a large heatproof bowl and beat until the sugar has dissolved and the mixture is thick and creamy.

• Return the infused milk to the heat and bring to a simmer. Put the cornstarch into a small bowl, then add 4 tablespoons of the infused milk and blend to a smooth paste. Stir the cornstarch paste into the simmering infused milk and cook over medium-low heat, stirring constantly, for 1 minute.

• Strain the milk mixture into the egg mixture and whisk until well blended. Rinse out the pan and put a small amount of water in the bottom. Bring the water to a simmer over medium-high heat. Reduce the heat to low, then set the bowl over the pan and heat, stirring constantly, for 25–30 minutes, or until the custard is thick enough to coat the back of the spoon—the water must not touch the bottom of the bowl or the eggs might scramble.

• Divide the mixture between 6 x 4-inch/10-cm round earthenware serving dishes, called *cazuelas* in Spain, or flat, white French crème brûlée dishes. Let cool completely, then cover and let chill in the refrigerator for at least 12 hours.

• To serve, sprinkle the top of each dessert with a thin layer of the remaining sugar. In Catalonia, the tops are caramelized with a special flat iron that is heated in a gas flame and then placed on top of the sugar. Unless you happen to have one of these, use a kitchen blowtorch—a broiler isn't hot enough. Let stand while the caramel hardens, then serve. The caramel will remain firm for about 1 hour at room temperature. Do not return to the refrigerator or the caramel will "melt."

SERVES 6
1 large egg, plus 3 large egg yolks
½ cup honey
1¼ cups heavy cream
3 pomegranates

"Jeweled" Honey Mousses

To make an orange version of these delicious mousses, add 2 teaspoons freshly grated orange rind with the honey in the second paragraph and decorate the tops of the mousses with thin strips of orange rind instead of the pomegranate seeds.

• Line 6 ramekins with pieces of plastic wrap large enough to extend over the tops. Set aside.
• Put the whole egg, egg yolks, and honey in a large bowl and beat until blended and fluffy. Beat the cream in a separate bowl until stiff peaks form. Fold the cream into the egg mixture.
• Divide the mixture evenly between the prepared ramekins, then fold the excess plastic wrap over the top of each. Freeze for at least 8 hours until firm. These mousses can be served directly from the freezer, because the texture is not solid.
• To serve, unfold the plastic wrap, then invert each ramekin onto a serving plate and remove the ramekin and plastic wrap. Cut the pomegranates in half and hold one half over each mousse in turn. Use your other hand to tap firmly on the base of the pomegranate so that the seeds fall over the mousse.

MAKES 1 X 10-INCH/25-CM TART
¾ cup/unsalted butter, at room
    temperature
scant 1 cup superfine sugar
3 large eggs
1¾ cups finely ground almonds
2 tsp all-purpose flour
1 tbsp finely grated orange rind
½ tsp almond extract

sifted confectioners' sugar,
    to decorate
sour cream (optional),
    to serve

PIE DOUGH
2 cups all-purpose flour, plus extra
    for dusting
generous ¾ cup superfine sugar
1 tsp finely grated lemon rind
pinch of salt
1⅜ sticks butter, diced and chilled
1 egg, lightly beaten
1 tbsp chilled water

Almond Tart

If you have difficulty rolling out this rich pie dough, roll it between two sheets of plastic wrap. Pull off the top sheet, then invert the dough into the pan and peel off the second sheet. Alternatively, roll the dough out in small pieces and "patch" them together with lightly floured fingers.

• First, make the pie dough. Sift the flour into a bowl and stir in the sugar, lemon rind, and salt. Add the butter and rub in with your fingertips until the mixture resembles fine bread crumbs. Mix the egg and water together in a pitcher, then slowly pour into the dry ingredients, stirring with a fork until the mixture comes together. Shape the dough into a ball and wrap in foil, then let chill in the refrigerator for at least 1 hour.

• Roll the dough out on a lightly floured counter to ⅛ inch/3 mm thick. Use to line a greased 10-inch/25-cm tart pan with a removable bottom. Chill the pastry shell in the refrigerator for at least 15 minutes. Meanwhile, preheat the oven to 425°F/220°C.

• Line the pastry shell with foil and fill with dried beans. Bake in the preheated oven for 12 minutes. Remove the foil and beans and bake for an additional 4 minutes, or until the pie dough has dried out. Remove from the oven and reduce the oven temperature to 400°F/200°C.

• Meanwhile, make the filling. Beat the butter and sugar in a bowl until creamy. Beat in the eggs, one at a time. Add the almonds, flour, orange rind, and almond extract and beat until blended.

• Spoon the filling into the pastry shell and smooth the surface. Bake in the preheated oven for 30–35 minutes, or until the top is golden and the tip of a knife inserted in the center comes out clean. Let cool completely on a cooling rack, then dust the top with sifted confectioners' sugar to decorate. Serve with a spoonful of sour cream, if you like.

SERVES 4–6

1 large orange

1 lemon

4 cups milk, plus extra if necessary

1¼ cups Spanish short-grain rice

½ cup superfine sugar

1 vanilla bean, split

pinch of salt

½ cup heavy cream

brown sugar, to serve (optional)

Spanish Rice Pudding

This thick, creamy dessert tastes equally good warm or chilled. You can serve it sprinkled with some lightly toasted chopped almonds or fine strips of orange rind, or with Poached Fruit Seville-Style or chopped Caramelized Almonds, instead of the brown sugar.

• Finely grate the rinds of the orange and lemon. Set aside. Rinse a heavy-bottom pan with cold water and do not dry it.

• Put the milk and rice in the pan and bring to a boil over medium-high heat. Reduce the heat, then stir in the superfine sugar, vanilla bean, orange and lemon rinds, and salt and let simmer, stirring frequently, until the pudding is thick and creamy and the rice grains are tender—this can take up to 30 minutes, depending on how wide the pan is.

• Remove the vanilla bean and stir in the cream. Serve immediately, sprinkled with brown sugar, if you like, or let cool completely, then cover and let chill in the refrigerator until required. The pudding will thicken as it cools, so stir in extra milk if necessary.

SERVES 4–6

1¼ cups blanched almonds
1¼ cups heavy cream
¼ tsp almond extract
⅔ cup light cream
½ cup confectioners' sugar

HOT CHOCOLATE SAUCE

3½ squares semisweet chocolate,
    broken into pieces
3 tbsp corn syrup
4 tbsp water
2 tbsp unsalted butter, diced
¼ tsp vanilla extract

Frozen Almond Cream with Hot Chocolate Sauce

If you don't have an ice-cream maker, put the mixture in a freezerproof container and freeze for 2 hours, or until it begins to thicken and freeze around the edges. Tip into a bowl and beat well. Return to the freezerproof container and freeze until almost frozen. Stir in the almonds and proceed with the third paragraph. You can make the sauce and the dessert in advance. Remove the dessert from the freezer 15 minutes before serving, and reheat the sauce gently.

• Preheat the oven to 400°F/200°C. Spread the almonds out on a cookie sheet and toast in the preheated oven, turning occasionally, for 8–10 minutes, or until golden brown and giving off a toasted aroma—watch carefully after 7 minutes because they quickly burn. Immediately tip onto a cutting board and let cool. Coarsely chop a scant ½ cup by hand and finely grind the remainder in a food processor or in a mortar with a pestle. Set both aside separately.

• Whip the heavy cream with the almond extract in a bowl until soft peaks form. Stir in the light cream and continue to whip, sifting in the sugar in 3 batches. Transfer to an ice-cream maker and freeze following the manufacturer's directions. When the cream is almost frozen, transfer to a bowl and stir in the chopped almonds so that they are evenly distributed.

• Put the cream mixture in a 1-lb/450-g loaf pan and smooth the surface. Wrap tightly in foil and freeze for at least 3 hours.

• To make the sauce, put the chocolate, syrup, and water in a heatproof bowl, then set the bowl over a pan of barely simmering water and heat, stirring, until the chocolate melts. Add the butter and vanilla extract and stir until smooth.

• To serve, unwrap the pan and dip the bottom in a sink of boiling water for just a couple of seconds. Invert onto a freezerproof tray, giving a sharp shake until the frozen cream drops out. Using a palette knife, coat the top and sides with the minced almonds. Return to the freezer unless serving immediately.

• Use a warm knife to slice into 8–12 slices. Arrange 2 slices on each plate and spoon the sauce around.

SERVES 4–6

3–4 lemons

generous 1 cup water

1 cup superfine sugar

1 bottle Spanish cava, chilled,
    to serve

Lemon Sherbet with Cava

Spaniards also serve lemon sherbet in frozen hollow lemon shells. To do this, slice the tops off 4–6 lemons and use a sharp teaspoon to scoop out the flesh. Spoon the almost-frozen sherbet into the lemons and place in the freezer upright until frozen.

• Roll the lemons on a counter, pressing firmly, to help extract as much juice as possible. Pare off a few strips of rind and set aside for decoration, if you like, then finely grate the rind of 3 lemons. Squeeze the juice from as many of the lemons as necessary to give ¾ cup and set aside.

• Put the water and sugar in a heavy-bottom pan over medium-high heat and stir until the sugar has dissolved. Bring to a boil, without stirring, and boil for 2 minutes. Remove from the heat and stir in the grated lemon rind. Cover and let stand for 30 minutes, or until cool.

• When the mixture is cool, stir in the lemon juice. Strain into an ice-cream maker and freeze according to the manufacturer's directions. Alternatively, strain the mixture into a freezerproof container and freeze for 2 hours, or until mushy and beginning to freeze around the edges. Tip into a bowl and beat well. Return to the freezerproof container and freeze for 2 hours. Repeat the process twice more. Remove the sherbet from the freezer 10 minutes before serving.

• To serve, scoop into 4–6 tall glasses, then decorate with the reserved lemon rind, if using, and top off with cava.

MAKES 12–15 GLASSES
generous ⅓ cup Spanish brandy
4 large lemons, sliced and cut
    into fourths
4 large oranges, sliced and cut
    into fourths
2 limes, sliced and cut into fourths

2 peaches, pitted and sliced (optional)
2 x 75-cl bottles full-bodied Spanish
    red wine, chilled
1 cup superfine sugar, plus extra
    to taste (optional)
ice cubes, to serve

Sangria

Sangria is a famous Spanish drink. You can vary the combinations of fruit according to taste and what is available. Try adding nectarines or plums, pitted and sliced, or seedless grapes, halved.

• Put the brandy and half the citrus fruit pieces and peach slices, if using, in a nonmetallic bowl and use a wooden spoon to crush the fruit into the brandy. Cover and let chill in the refrigerator for at least 2 hours. Cover the remaining fruit and let chill in the refrigerator until required.

• Pour the brandy and fruit into a large serving pitcher, then add the wine and sugar, and stir until the sugar has dissolved. Taste and add extra sugar, if you like. Put a mixture of the chilled fruit slices in glasses and pour over the Sangria, including some of the brandy-soaked fruit.

SERVES 4–6

3½ squares semisweet chocolate,
    with at least 70% cocoa solids,
    broken into pieces
2½ cups milk
generous ½ cup superfine sugar
3½ tbsp cornstarch
1 tsp vanilla extract
pinch salt

Hot Chocolate

Spaniards love their hot chocolate so thick that you almost need to eat it with a spoon. It is an ideal drink for dipping fried pastries and other delicacies. To add a warm, spicy flavor to this delicious drink, sprinkle a little ground cinnamon over the surface before serving.

• Melt the chocolate in the milk in a heavy-bottom pan over medium heat, stirring constantly. Add the sugar and stir until it has dissolved.

• Put the cornstarch in a small bowl and make a well in the center. Add about 2 tablespoons of the chocolate milk and gradually blend the cornstarch into the liquid until thick. Stir all the cornstarch mixture into the pan and bring to a simmer, stirring. Bring to a boil and cook, stirring constantly, until the mixture thickens. Pour into coffee cups and serve immediately.

Index